My Nanny a

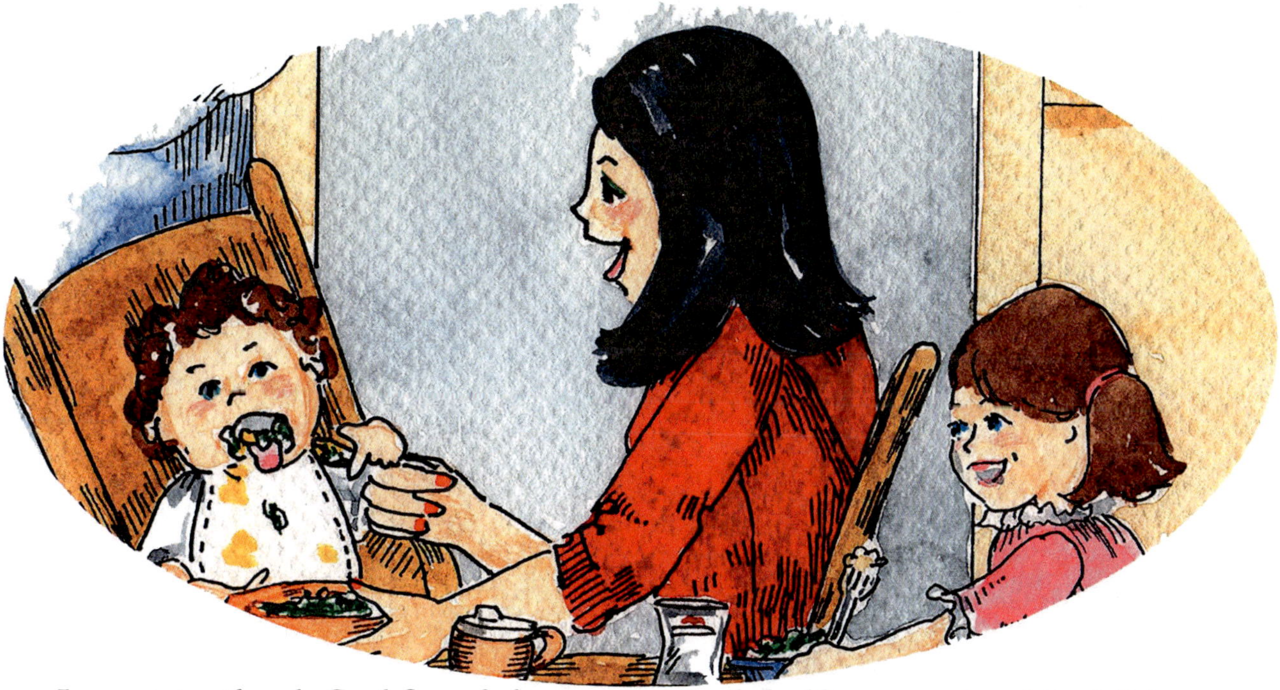

I want to thank God for giving me a special gift to work with children.

For Malachi, with Love.

DanniNanny Publishing Co.
Delaware
Email. allforkids08@yahoo.com

www.LaurieBarrows.com

A B C D E F G H I J K

**Hi, I'm Olivia and this is baby Michael.
I want to tell you about our nanny.
My nanny takes care of us while
Mommy and Daddy go to work.**

In the morning, she fixes my favorite breakfast – Pancakes, Strawberries, and Orange Juice. Michael eats baby food – Cereal and drinks a bottle.

NOTICE
Grain
Flour
MAX

After breakfast I get dressed.

Then, I brush my teeth.

My nanny likes to play puzzles and do arts and crafts with me. My baby brother plays with his toys (they make silly sounds). I love when my nanny reads to us. She likes to make silly animal sounds too. When we make a big mess, my nanny says, “Clean up time”.

PUZZLE
games

Later in the day, my nanny plans fun play dates. Today, we are playing with Jonathan and his nanny. Our nannies are taking us to the park. At the park, I play on the jungle gym and my nanny carries my brother around. I met some new friends; they were really nice to me.

After the park,
my nanny takes
us to the zoo.
I am so excited!

While we are at the zoo, we get our faces painted. Our nannies are laughing.

After we finish looking and playing with the animals, we eat lunch. I am having a turkey and cheese sandwich with apple sauce. Jonathan is eating a grilled cheese sandwich and a banana.
After lunch we leave the zoo. My baby brother needs a nap.

1:15

PUZZLE
game

When we make it home, my nanny lays Michael down for his nap. Today, we are making ABC's with Cheerios. I love gluing. After arts and crafts, we read a few books. Sometimes I like to read to my nanny.
She always says I do a good job.
Uh oh! I think I hear my brother crying.
We need to get him out of his crib.

Now it's dinner time. We are having chicken, broccoli and fruit. Umm, sounds yummy!
My brother is eating baby food.
When dinner is over, I help my nanny clean up and get ready for bath time.

NOTICE
PUPPY
FOOD
Grain
Flour
MAX

My brother and I take baths together. He stays in the baby tub. I am taking a bubble bath in the big tub. I love playing with my rubbie ducky. After bath time, we put on our pajamas.

My nanny does not have to help me. I put my pajamas on like a BIG GIRL.
After I put on my pajamas, I go back to the bathroom to brush my teeth. Soon, mommy and daddy will be home and my nanny will leave.

I love it when mommy and daddy come home because I can tell them about my busy day with my nanny.

About the Author

I have worked in the childcare industry for over 11 years and have been a professional nanny for six years. Most people know me as DanniNanny. During my career as a professional nanny, I have been asked over and over again to explain what a nanny is and what a nanny does.

My Nanny and Me **is my chance to tell children and parents about nannies. Children have always been special to me, and I have been blessed to work with so many families and touch the lives of so many children. To all the children I have nannied and babysat over the years -**
THANK YOU & I LOVE YOU ALL!

Made in United States
North Haven, CT
28 May 2022